A STEP BY STEP BOOK ABOUT
GUINEA PIGS

ANMARIE BARRIE

Photography: Glen S. Axelrod, Michael Gilroy, Brian Seed, Sally Anne Thompson, David Whiteway.

Humorous drawings by Andrew Prendimano.

Distributed in the UNITED STATES by T.F.H. Publications, Inc., 211 West Sylvania Avenue, Neptune City, NJ 07753; in CANADA to the Book Trade by Macmillan of Canada (A Division of Canada Publishing Corporation), 164 Commander Boulevard, Agincourt, Ontario M1S 3C7; in ENGLAND by T.F.H. Publications Limited, 4 Kier Park, Ascot, Berkshire SL5 7DS; in AUSTRALIA AND THE SOUTH PACIFIC by T.F.H. (Australia) Pty. Ltd., Box 149, Brookvale 2100 N.S.W., Australia; in NEW ZEALAND by Ross Haines & Son, Ltd., 18 Monmouth Street, Grey Lynn, Auckland 2, New Zealand; in SINGAPORE AND MALAYSIA by MPH Distributors (S) Pte., Ltd., 601 Sims Drive, #03/07/21, Singapore 1438; in the PHILIPPINES by Bio-Research, 5 Lippay Street, San Lorenzo Village, Makati Rizal; in SOUTH AFRICA by Multipet Pty. Ltd., 30 Turners Avenue, Durban 4001. Published by T.F.H. Publications, Inc. Manufactured in the United States of America by T.F.H. Publications, Inc.

Contents

INTRODUCTION

Guinea pigs, or cavies, are small mammals classified as rodents, a category which includes mice, gerbils, hamsters, and domestic rats, among others. All mammals have a four-chambered heart, have hair, give birth to live young, and feed their babies with their own milk. Guinea pigs, though, are not as prolific as their rodent cousins. In fact, comparatively, guinea pig offspring are few and far between. Another difference is that guinea pigs have no external tail. Like all rodents, guinea pigs have continually growing incisor teeth that are worn down from chewing.

Wild guinea pigs (*Cavia aperea* and *tschudii)* originate in South America. Due to their great ability to adapt, they are found in a wide range of habitats. These include swamps, rocky areas, savannas, and the edges of forests. From Colombia and Venezuela down to Brazil and northern Argentina, guinea pigs live in low to high terrains and dry to moist climates. They are active in the daytime, feeding on the local vegetation of grasses and the flesh of cacti. These wild specimens have a dark, muddy-colored fur. Kept as pets by the native Indians of Peru, they were prized for their meat as well as their fur.

Sixteenth century slave traders imported guinea pigs to Europe from South America. On these voyages, the ships stopped at the West African coast of Guinea, so many Europeans may have thought that the animals came from this region: hence the name "guinea." Or, because they were exported from Guiana in South America, people may have confused the named Guiana with the more familiar Guinea. "Pig" may have come about because male guinea pigs are called "boars" while

FACING PAGE:
Guinea pigs are superb pets; they're cute and lovable with endearing personalities.

females are referred to as "sows." However, babies are known as "pups," not piglets. Whatever the origin of the name, these affectionate little creatures, "shaped like a brick with the corners chopped off," became popular European pets.

Domesticated guinea pigs *(Cavia porcellus)* differ from their wild relatives because of their rounder, plumper heads and bodies. They also come in an exceptionally wide variety of coat and color types.

In addition to being superb pets, guinea pigs are used extensively in research laboratories and hospitals. Their ease of care and ability to breed rapidly make them ideal for the study of heredity. Many schools keep guinea pigs so that the children learn about caring for a dependent creature and experience firsthand the processes of life, growth, reproduction, and death.

Frequently, animal experts and enthusiasts correctly refer to guinea pigs as "cavies." (Remember that the name guinea pig is actually a misnomer.) Even though "cavies" is the more accurate term, do not be surprised if the average person,

This is a show quality Chocolate boar guinea pig.

even a pet shop employee, is not familiar with this name.

Guinea pigs make wonderful pets for people of all ages for a multitude of reasons.

When fully grown, a guinea pig will be eight to ten inches long, about four inches high, and will weigh from one to three pounds. Their small size means that they are easy to handle and fondle. In fact, guinea pigs respond well to cuddling and hugging. Often an animal will settle comfortably in your lap to be petted and scratched.

Domesticated guinea pigs come in an exceptionally wide variety of coat and color types.

Not only are these pets cute and lovable; they also have endearing personalities. They are gentle, friendly, and will not bite, even if handled roughly or improperly. Unfortunately, guinea pigs cannot be housebroken and may therefore leave you a little wet.

Guinea pigs are vocal animals, so they will whistle and purr enthusiastically to their owner. Some will even lick their human friends as a type of kiss.

Guinea pigs are not expensive. Their diet is simple, the food is not costly, and their housing can be bought or cheaply made. Since they require a minimum of space, they can be safely kept in apartments or small houses that do not readily lend themselves to other larger domestic animals.

Since guinea pigs are clean by nature, their housing demands little maintenance to keep it clean and odor-free. Another advantage is that guinea pigs are hardy animals and should remain relatively free of disease (with the proper care)

A Self White cavy. This show cavy has good ears; they are well shaped and not crinkled at the edges.

Guinea pigs make excellent pets! Everybody wants to pet these lovable little "critters."

throughout their lifetime. And because guinea pigs do not breed as often as other rodents and their litters are smaller, you don't have to be concerned about being quickly overrun should you choose to breed your pet. In addition, the wide range of colors and hair types common to guinea pigs offers both the amateur hobbyist and the professional breeder a rewarding challenge.

Unlike some other pets, guinea pigs do not require vaccinations for diseases like distemper and rabies, nor do they need to be licensed.

Because guinea pigs are small and their housing is compact, they are easily transported. You will find it surprisingly entertaining to take them along on family trips.

For all of these reasons, plus a few others that you can probably think of, guinea pigs are excellent pets for youngsters, invalids, and even adults! Some fortunate owners have had the love and companionship of their pet guinea pigs for more than seven years.

Breeds and Varieties

There are presently seven breeds of guinea pigs recognized by the American Cavy Breeders Association and the American Rabbit Breeders Association. The animals are further classified by color, hair type, and hair length to determine the variety. A Standard of Perfection, which outlines the ideals for showing and breeding, can be ordered from the American Rabbit Breeders Association. This Standard of Perfection exemplifies the type, fur, color, markings, and condition of each variety of guinea pig, as well as listing the faults and disqualifications for showing.

Top view of a dark Tri-colored Peruvian sow. The head furnishings, or frontal fringe, the sidesweeps, and backsweep are balanced in their lengths.

Introduction

Cavies come in several colors and hair types. An adult guinea pig is about the size of a young rabbit.

Although there are many varieties of guinea pigs, the best known and most readily obtainable are: the American short-haired, the Peruvian long-haired, and the Abyssinian rough-haired.

Breeds
THE AMERICAN OR ENGLISH

The American is probably the best known and most widely raised strain. The hair is short, smooth, finely textured, and highly glossed. Counting all possible combinations, the American comes in thirty-six colors! The range includes mixed and solid white, black, brown, chocolate, red, beige, cream, lilac, silver, and golden. Used extensively in research laboratories and hospitals, the white (or albino) American guinea pigs are the most commonly raised by commercial breeders.

Averaging a bit over two pounds, the American should exhibit broad shoulders, a wide nose, open ears, a long body, rounded rump, and a high, full crown. (The crown is the rounded bulge above the neck and shoulders.) The ears should be slightly drooped and the eyes should match the body color. In show animals, the feet should also match the body color.

Because of their easy-going temperaments, American guinea pigs will sit contentedly in your lap. They are also an extremely hardy breed, and their short coat requires little care.

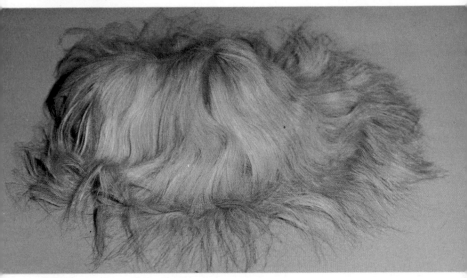

The hair on this Golden Peruvian Sow can grow as long as twenty inches or more.

THE ABYSSINIAN

The distinguishing feature of the Abyssinian is its harsh, wiry coat, similar to that of a wire terrier. This rough hair emanates from cowlicks, swirling into well-formed and distinct rosettes. The more rosettes present on the animal, the better, as long as they are round and separate, with no overlapping. In competition, the rosettes are actually counted. Regular grooming will enhance the condition of the coat.

Abyssinians weigh an average of two pounds. In comparison to other guinea pigs, their eyes tend to be less round and less pronounced. Their ears stand out sideways a bit more, and they display a collar of stiff, erect hairs around the shoulders and across the hindquarters. A well-defined ridge of hair also runs along the cheeks.

This guinea pig breed tends to have a high-strung and lively disposition. The Abyssinians are rather vocal, demanding, and charmingly independent. Some owners praise them as the most intelligent of all guinea pig breeds.

Introduction

THE PERUVIAN

Usually considered show stock, the Peruvian has straight silky hair covering the entire body. Some notable specimens have attained a hair length of twenty inches or more! Although Peruvians are bred in an assortment of colors and patterns, it is the length of the coat that is considered the most important aspect of their striking beauty.

The coat should part from the spine and cascade down the sides of the animal like a mane. At first glance, it should be difficult to determine which end of the guinea pig is which.

To keep the fur free of tangles it should be brushed and combed daily. At least once a month the hair needs to be washed and set to remain in prime condition. Also, the Peruvian must be protected more diligently from drafts and colds than other breeds. Therefore, a hardier breed, and one that requires less attentive grooming, should be considered for the first guinea pig.

THE SILKIE OR SHELTIE

A mutation of the Peruvian, the Silkie is another long-haired breed. The silky-textured coat grows straight back to the rump without a part and it comes in all colors.

This Abyssinian Brindle boar's coat has a number of distinct cowlicks. Many consider these independent animals the most intelligent of all guinea pig breeds.

THE TEDDY

A relatively new breed, the Teddy has a kinky coat that is about one-half inch long, like that of a teddy bear.

THE WHITE CRESTED

Similar to the American in appearance and temperament, the White Crested has a single white rosette on the top of the head. (No other white areas can be present on the body of a show animal.)

THE SATIN

The Satin resembles the American and the White Crested, with its distinguishing feature being the satin-like coat. The coat has a translucent quality due to the small diameter of each hair shaft. This results in the satiny, glass-like appearance.

Color Types

AGOUTI

Named after a South American rodent, the coat of the Agouti guinea pig resembles that of the wild agouti. Each hair shaft has two colors: the tip and base of the shafts are the same color, with a band of contrasting color in the middle. This barring gives the coat a ticked effect.

The three recognized Agouti colors are golden, silver, and cinnamon.

SELF

Selfs have a solid color coat. Because it is easier to produce a coat of one color than it is to produce patterns or markings, these guinea pigs are the most popular and most widely bred. They are available in beige, blue, chocolate, cream, lilac, red, white, golden, and black. Often the eye color matches the body color.

SOLID

The Solids have mixed hair color on the entire body. The types include the Brindle, Dilute, Golden, Silver, and Roan.

MARKED

Marked guinea pigs are a combination of two or more colors. The markings are clear and distinct, arranged in a specific pattern. Each patch of color is sharp and clean, not mixed. Understandably, this variety is quite a challenge to the breeder. The Dutch, Himalayan, Broken Color, Dalmatian, Tortoise Shell, and Tortoise-Shell-and-White are all well-known types.

This is a prime example of the Agouti guinea pig.

SELECTING YOUR CAVY

Such a wide range of guinea pigs is available that you may find it difficult to choose from among them. Of course, you'll have to bear in mind how you intend to use the animal. If you plan to show, then pick a beautiful specimen which meets its Standard of Perfection as closely as possible. For breeding purposes, a guinea pig has to be of the proper age in addition to possessing desirable traits. As a pet, one that has a good disposition and that requires little grooming is probably the best choice. Whatever guinea pig you select, though, has to appeal to you. If you don't see the one that you want, speak to the dealer. It is likely that he can order a specific guinea pig for you. Select the best animal you can find because the care, feeding, and maintenance are the same no matter what the quality of the pet.

Most importantly, your guinea pig needs to be fit. Sick and weak animals demand far greater care and attention. Diseases also have a more damaging effect on an unhealthy body. Ill guinea pigs can transmit infections to the rest of your stock and, of course, they should never be used as breeders.

Patronize a pet shop that has knowledgeable employees who can offer sound advice. These are the people to rely on when you need help. A dealer with a long-standing record of good stock won't sell an unfit animal which may mar his reputation. His store should have clean, neat cages, healthy guinea pigs, and a well-stocked inventory. Here you can purchase your pet and all the supplies that go with it. One-stop shopping is a great convenience.

Look for a guinea pig that is completely weaned from

FACING PAGE:
These cuddly cream and buff guinea pigs are just waiting to be taken to a good home with some lucky new owner.

its mother, about six to eight weeks old. Young guinea pigs are curious and playful, ready to adapt to new surroundings. The eyes should be bright, and the animal should have an alert appearance. No watery discharge should be present around the eyes or nose. The fur should be full and shiny, with no bare spots anywhere on the body.

Extend your hand toward a particular guinea pig. It should seem curious and somewhat suspicious, but not run wildly about the cage. A well-tempered guinea will tame easily. One more nervous and high-strung may not be as good a pet, yet can still be fine for breeding. Keep in mind that although disposition tends to run in strains, it makes little difference whether you get a male or a female for a pet. However, if you plan to purchase a pair of guinea pigs (other than for breeding), get two females. They tend to be more compatible than males, who are likely to fight.

Without any sudden or abrupt actions, grasp the guinea pig firmly about the shoulders. Support the hindquarters with your other hand, lifting the animal so that the belly faces up. Supporting the guinea pig properly makes it feel secure and reduces struggling and possible injury.

The guinea pig should feel full and solid in your hands, weighing between eight and twelve ounces. The head and shoulders should be broad, and the ears should droop slightly. If the animal has a pot belly, or if the ribs protrude, make another selection.

Look inside the ears. No scabs or scales should be present. Check the teeth. They should come together nicely, and no teeth should be broken. Tooth troubles can result in a guinea pig not being able to eat properly.

Observe the guinea pig in its cage for as long as possible. It should have an active, lively spirit, and be able to run swiftly and smoothly. The back line of the body should remain level as the animal moves. If it bounces up and down, there may be a problem with the legs.

You may decide to have your pet examined by a veterinarian before bringing it home. Make an arrangement with the shopkeeper for a refund or exchange if the veterinarian declares the guinea pig unfit.

Sexing

When forming male-female pairs, or when segregating the weaned young, you may need to determine the sex of your guinea pigs. At first, you may have some difficulty.

Lift the guinea pig under the chest and raise it so the head and shoulders rest against your body. Support the rear with your other hand. In the genital area, both the male and female have a slit shaped like an inverted 'Y'. Gently press in front of this slit. The penis will appear in the middle of the 'Y' if the guinea pig is a male. However, this technique should never be performed on any guinea pig less than three weeks old.

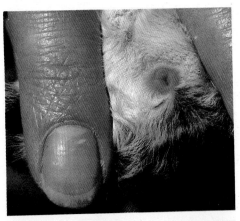

UPPER PHOTO: In the young boar, the penis will appear in the middle of the 'Y'.
LOWER PHOTO: Female guinea pig. Sexing technique should not be attempted until the guinea pig is over three weeks old.

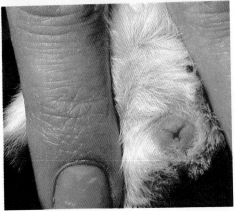

The cage, its accessories, and your guinea pig's food should all be arranged in advance before bringing your new pet home. Your guinea pig may be understandably nervous, so having its residence prepared in advance will ease the transition. Immediately upon arrival the animal can be secure, comfortable, and well-fed.

EQUIPMENT

To further diminish the stress of travel, do not transport the guinea pig on a cold, windy, or damp day. The more protection and consideration you give your pet, the less chance of illness and accidents.

If you already have guinea pigs at home, isolate the new arrival in another room for thirty days. Quarantining allows for the detection and treatment of infectious diseases before they are transmitted to the rest of the colony.

Housing

The type of housing you choose for your guinea pig should be as large as you can afford, comfortably accommodating, and easy to clean. All accommodations need to be clean, dry, safe, draft-free, and well-ventilated.

It is almost always better to buy the first cage, pen, or hutch than it is to build one yourself. Mass manufacturers can produce them faster, sturdier, and less expensively. In addition, they have probably worked out bugs that you never even thought of. After some experience with ready-made housing, you can modify and adapt the standard designs to suit your particular needs.

The minimum size requirement for a single guinea pig is two square feet of floor space. For it to be happy and con-

FACING PAGE:
The guinea pig you choose, like this beautiful
American crested smooth-haired cavy, should be
alert, with bright eyes and a lively spirit.

tent, a guinea pig needs plenty of room for exercise. This doesn't mean that the quarters have to be fancy, just roomy. Ladders and stairways connecting the floor to an upper shelf increase an animal's mobility. You'll discover that your guinea pig will relish climbing ramps, poising on shelves, and snuggling under things.

Guinea pigs are sensitive to fluctuations in temperature, so be sure to maintain a relatively constant temperature. Ideal is between 68 and 72 degrees F, which minimizes colds

Choose the largest cage you can afford so your cavy will have plenty of room to exercise.

and other illnesses. Above 90°, heat prostration may occur. Below 55 degrees, the reproduction rate slows, the litter size decreases, and the young grow poorly. Also, do not place an indoor cage near a drafy window or door where drastic changes in temperature are likely.

An assortment of metal cages is available on the market. Metal is durable, chew resistant, and easy to clean. Avoid painted cages because the epoxy may be toxic to your pet.

A happy guinea pig has a supply of clean, fresh water all the time. A water bottle like this one won't spill, and the water stays clean.

Wooden cages are also not recommended because they are more difficult to maintain. Parasites harbor in the nooks and crannies and, when saturated with urine, the wood can become foul-smelling. Guinea pigs like to gnaw, so a wooden cage is soon splintered and weakened. Since wooden cages need to be replaced more often than metal, they are more expensive in the long run.

A cage can be entirely metal or a combination of metal and hard plastic. The floor should be solid, not wire. Wire flooring may make a guinea pig's feet and hocks tender. Toes can be caught, and the open grid allows precious heat to escape through the bottom of the cage. If you happen to select a cage with a wire floor, simply remove it to use the solid bottom.

A well-made cage will probably come with a removable plastic or metal tray at the bottom which slides out like a drawer for easy cleaning. Many cage models are also equipped with feed and water dishes and a shelf for your pet to climb on. A variety of standard cages manufactured for other small mammals are quite well-suited to guinea pigs.

Since food and bedding material can be tossed out of the cage and scattered about, you might like to line the lower three inches of the cage with a border of fine wire mesh or a plastic shield. This helps to confine the cage contents. A plastic-metal cage has this feature built in.

A large glass aquarium (minimum twenty gallons) makes for adequate housing. "Leakers" and used tanks can often be bought for a reasonable price in pet shops. Be sure, however, never to set an aquarium in an area of direct sunlight. The temperature within may get so high that a guinea pig can suffer from heat prostration.

Cavies are naturally clean animals; to help them along there are several ammonia-absorbing products available at your pet store.

Equipment

Both of these guinea pigs are white—but the long-haired guinea pig (Abyssinian) is an albino, while the dark-eyed cavy is not.

Guinea pigs do not climb much or jump, and they rarely attempt to escape. Therefore, a cage lid is not mandatory. However, the walls need to be high enough to give an illusion of confinement. In addition, you may think it wise to provide a roof that *protects* your guinea pig from undisciplined children and investigating animals.

Your guinea pig's home should be positioned on a sturdy table or stand about three feet above the ground. This height saves you a lot of stretching and bending as you clean, feed, or simply observe your pet. It also protects against floor drafts and curious pets.

If you plan to raise a great number of guinea pigs, first visit some local breeders. This will give you valuable insight as to the types of materials and housing arrangements best suited to your area. In most breeding colonies, pens are tiered to increase the number of guinea pigs that can be bred and raised per square unit of floor space. These tiers can be arranged in steps or stacked directly over one another.

Bedding

Proper bedding aids in keeping your guinea pig dry, warm, clean, and comfortable. Spread an inch deep over the cage floor, the bedding needs to be dust-free, fluffy, absorbent, and non-staining. Materials such as chaff, peanut shells, wood shavings, peat moss, and crushed corn cobs are all good choices. Hay and straw are acceptable, but guinea pigs like to nibble the hay even once it is soiled. Needless to say, this can make an animal quite ill. In addition, hay and straw soon get wet and need to be replaced often. Sawdust scatters and sticks to fur when it is dry. When the sawdust is wet, it mats down quite firmly. Newspaper is not advisable because the ink stains the coat. Also, if a guinea pig eats the paper, the lead in the ink will make it sick.

Cleaning Your Guinea Pig's Home

To keep your guinea pig healthy and its quarters odor-free, clean out the soiled corner of the cage each day. (Fortunately, most guinea pigs select one corner of the cage to use

If you use hay for your guinea pig's bedding, be sure to change it often.

A frightened guinea pig will remain still and huddled.

regularly as their "toilet.") Then at least once a week replace the bedding entirely. Periodically scrub the floor and the cage with a mild disinfectant, such as one used to deodorize kitty litter pans. Rinse the cage well and allow it to dry thoroughly before refilling it with fresh bedding and re-introducing your pet.

While you clean, your guinea pig can be kept securely out of the way in a box or small cage. A room with no means of escape and no potential hazards is another alternative.

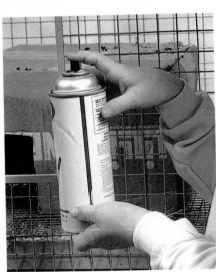

Clean the cage often and use a mild disinfectant before refilling with fresh bedding.

Nutrients are important chemical substances that work together and interact with the body chemicals to perform one or more of the following functions: to provide materials to build, repair, and maintain body tissues; to supply substances that function in the regulation of body processes; and to furnish the fuel needed for energy.

NUTRITION

The nutrients needed by the body are usually available in food. It is the nutrients in food (protein, carbohydrates, fats, vitamins, minerals, and water), not specific foods, which are needed.

The digestive system processes foods into nutrients or nutrient combinations and waste products. Blood carries these nutrients from the digestive system and oxygen from the air breathed to every cell in the body. Some nutrients need to be replenished every day from the foods eaten; others can be stored in the body for future use.

Each nutrient has certain special jobs to do in the building, maintenance, and operation of the body. These jobs cannot be done by other nutrients. In other words, an extra supply of one cannot make up for a shortage of another. Other jobs in the body require nutrients to work together as a team.

Protein constitutes part of the structure of every cell, including muscle, blood, and bone. Throughout life, protein is required: to support growth and maintain healthy body cells; to make hemoglobin, which carries oxygen to the cells; to form antibodies in the bloodstream to increase resistance to infection; and to produce enzymes, hormones, and body fluids that regulate body processes. Protein may also be used to supply energy.

FACING PAGE:
Guinea pigs really enjoy fresh vegetables as a supplement to their diets.
But make sure that fresh vegetables don't form a major part of their diet.

Carbohydrates are the major source of energy for the red blood cells and the central nervous system. Carbohydrates spare protein from being used for energy, freeing it for vital functions such as growth and maintenance of body cells. Unrefined products supply fiber or roughage — complex carbohydrates — for regular elimination. Carbohydrates also aid in fat utilization.

Constituting part of the structure of every cell, fat is a concentrated dietary source of energy. It supplies essential fatty acids and carries Vitamins A, D, E, and K. Fat helps the body use protein and carbohydrates more efficiently. It is a component of cell walls. Deposits of fat serve to heat, support, and protect from injury the vital organs.

Vitamins function primarily as catalysts in chemical reactions within the body. They are essential for the release of energy within the body, for tissue building, and for controlling the body's use of food. By themselves, vitamins do not supply

This adorable white guinea pig has a single rosette or whorl on the head; it is recognized as a crested guinea pig.

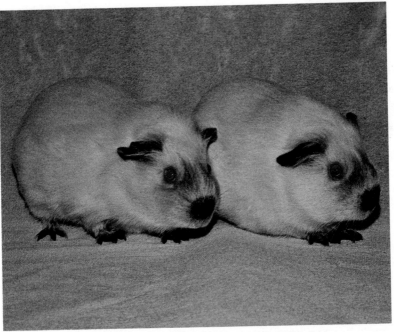

These young Himalayan cavies are well fed and healthy-looking.

energy or build tissues. Each vitamin serves one or more functions in the body that no other nutrient can. An inadequacy of a minute amount of a vitamin can have disastrous effects on body processes and health.

Vitamin A has a role in the building of body cells. It is necessary for the growth of the young and the development of babies before birth. Needed for bone growth and healthy tooth structure, Vitamin A promotes good vision and prevents certain eye diseases. Vitamin A also assists in the formation and maintenance of skin and mucous membranes that line body cavities and tracts, such as the nasal passages and intestinal tract, thus increasing resistance to infection.

The vitamins in the B complex are important for growth, crucial to the metabolism of fats and carbohydrates, and vital for the maintenance of the nervous system. Niacin aids in the utilization of energy. It functions as part of a coenzyme in fat synthesis, tissue respiration, and the use of carbohydrates. Niacin promotes healthy skin and nerves, and aids digestion to foster a normal appetite.

Vitamin C plays a role in the formation and maintenance of collagen, which holds body cells together, thus strengthening blood vessels, hastening the healing of wounds and bones, and increasing resistance to infection. Vitamin C is also important for healthy gums, sound bones and teeth, and as an aid in the utilization of iron.

Guinea pig pellets are excellent nutrition for your animal; supplement them with occasional fresh treats for a healthy, happy pet.

Like vitamins, minerals do not supply calories. They are not broken down in the digestive process, but are partly absorbed, if soluable, for use in about the same forms as they occur in foods. Minerals, except iron, are not used up in the body but are excreted after carrying out their particular functions. Losses must be replenished regularly by the foods ingested.

Water is an important nutrient, essential for life. (You may be surprised to learn that water is considered a nutrient.) Water serves as a building material, a solvent, and a regulator

The markings of a Himalayan guinea pig correspond to those found in a Himalayan rabbit.

of body temperature. It carries nutrients to cells and waste products away. It aids digestion and is necessary in all chemical reactions in metabolism. The dietary sources of water include not only liquids, but also the moisture in foods.

Feeding

Fortunately for us, almost all of a guinea pig's nutritional requirements have been combined in one convenient form known as the guinea pig pellet. No home mixture could be more nutritious, convenient, or less expensive. These pellets

Alfalfa is delicious (to guinea pigs) and a very healthy dietary supplement. Your pet shop will be able to supply as much as you need.

are designed to meet the scientific ratio of requirements, supplemented only by green foods and water. Be sure, though, to read the label intently to ensure all the criteria have been met. After all, pellets do vary from brand to brand.

Guinea pig pellets can be purchased at pet shops. Do not accept pellets marked for other animals because their ingredients differ from those designed for guinea pigs. For example, rabbit pellets lack vitamin C, a nutrient that guinea pigs cannot produce internally as rabbits do.

Buy only a few weeks' supply of pellets at a time. By ninety days the food has lost most of its nutritional value. Seal the pellets in moisture-proof containers kept in a cool, dark, dry area. These precautions guard against humidity and moisture which foster harmful molds.

Once a day, a small amount of green food (fruits and vegetables) should be offered. Too ample a supply can result in diarrhea. Do not treat your guinea pig to foods that are not as

fresh as what you yourself would eat, even though a guinea pig will probably not eat something that is not good for it. The greens should be presented early in the day and removed before nightfall because foods left overnight will be spoiled by the morning.

Fresh tomatoes, cabbage, carrots and their tops, string beans, potatoes, apples, spinach, and many more fruits and vegetables will be welcomed by your pet. Even vegetation from around your home, like clover, dandelions, and lawn clippings, can be offered. Just be sure that the area has not been sprayed with insecticides or fouled by other animals. Of course, all fresh foods should be washed thoroughly to remove the dirt and contaminants.

You may be able to work out an arrangement with your local grocer to regularly pick up his produce scraps. This not only guarantees a fresh supply of greens the year 'round, but may save you a few dollars as well!

This guinea pig is really enjoying his daily lettuce leaf—and it's good for him.

Give your guinea pig new food sparingly, and introduce only one type at a time. Too sudden a change in the diet may cause a stomach upset. Presenting your pet with this variety of greens allows it to develop its own tastes. Soon you'll be able to recognize some of its favorites to be offered as special treats.

Hay is a good source of dietary roughage and the stems can be used for bedding. You should make a little holder for the hay or clip it to a cage bar with a clothespin so that it won't be contaminated with droppings. (Other fresh foods can be clipped in this manner.) Alfalfa hay cubes serve the same purpose as well.

It's a good idea to offer a salt lick for your cavy; he will decide whether he needs it or not.

Food can be set in earthenware or metal bowls with heavy bases, and too small for a guinea pig to sit in. Plastic dishes can be chewed and tipped readily. An alternative feeding device is a feed hopper that fastens to the outside of the cage. The food drops into a trough from which the animal can feed.

If water is provided in a bowl, your guinea pig may upset the dish, contaminate the water with food and droppings, or sit in the container. To prevent these possibilities from occurring, offer the liquid in a gravity-flow water bottle with a metal tube. Since guinea pigs chew and tug at the end of the

A tame cavy will happily take a hand-fed treat from his owner. Carrots are good for guinea pigs if fed only as occasional treats.

tube instead of merely licking it, plastic is unsuitable and glass unsafe. Also, your guinea pig will blow water back up the tube, causing the contents to become slimy. Therefore, freshen the water and disinfect the bottle daily.

Once your guinea pig has settled in and developed a routine, monitor its food and water intake over a week. An average adult eats about one third of a cup or two ounces of pellets and drinks roughly four to six ounces of water a day. In the future, you will be able to note any dietary changes that may indicate disease or injury.

HANDLING

Much of the fun in having a guinea pig is being able to hug, caress, and love it. In fact, your pet will respond positively to all the attention and affection you give it.

If you have never handled small animals before, you may be somewhat hesitant about reaching into the cage to pick up the guinea pig. Rest assured, though, that guinea pigs very seldom bite. During these initial handling sessions your pet will be more fearful of you than you are of it!

An untame guinea pig will scamper wildly about the cage upon the intrusion of an unfamiliar hand. Be aware that a guinea pig is also one of the fastest "backer-uppers" around. Don't let this animal's skittishness intimidate you.

To stop the guinea pig's dashing about, gently edge it into a corner and place one of your hands over its shoulders. Slip your other hand underneath the body, then slide your top hand from the shoulders down to the buttocks. For security, use both hands to slowly raise the animal. A guinea pig must always be safeguarded from falls because it cannot flip itself over in the air to land feet first the way cats do. Bruises and broken bones often result from falls.

Once lifted, there are several ways to hold the guinea pig, and your pet may show a personal preference. First, it can relax on your hand and forearm as you rest it next to your body. Second, you can cradle the guinea pig, belly up, in the crook of your arm, much as you would an infant. Third, your guinea pig may like its head up, with its belly and chest against you. One hand needs to support the hindquarters while the other rests on the back.

FACING PAGE
Remember to use both hands to support the full weight of the guinea pig when holding it.

The important thing to remember when holding a guinea pig is to always support its full weight. Don't leave the feet hanging out or cause the guinea pig to twist and struggle. Providing a feeling of security will allow the animal to relax in your arms. Never grab a guinea pig by the feet or the neck.

Training

Allow your guinea pig some time to adjust to its new surroundings. Set the cage in an area of moderate activity so the animal becomes familiar with the household activity. For the first few days do not attempt to touch the animal. Simply approach the cage slowly, all the while whistling and speaking softly to keep your pet calm. When the guinea pig appears to have settled in a bit, introduce your hand into the cage permitting the animal to sniff all around. Gently stroke the guinea pig, and soon you will be able to lift it out of the cage without too much fuss.

Although a guinea pig may not be as quick to perform tricks as some other animals do, with plenty of time and patience your pet can master a few simple tasks.

Guinea pigs are able to learn simple tricks, but it takes time and patience. Never punish a guinea pig!

The baby of this look-alike mother and son guinea pig pair is only a few weeks old. Guinea pig babies are born furred and capable of running around. They nurse only for a short time but during that brief period they are dependent on the mother, following her closely about. Guinea pig litters are small.

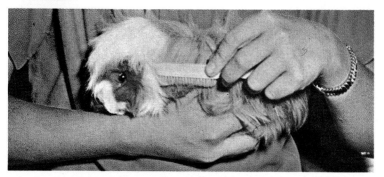

This cavy seems to be thoroughly enjoying his brushing.

The best training method involves positive reinforcement of the desired behavior and ignoring everything else. This technique demands a great amount of repetition with rewards of praise and food.

It is possible for you to get your pet to perform some natural behaviors on command. Many owners have taught their guinea pigs to sit up and whistle, run around in circles, and to follow them when they call the animal by name. Just be patient, and use your imagination!

Some of the longer-haired breeds of cavy require more grooming for their coats to stay beautiful and tangle-free.

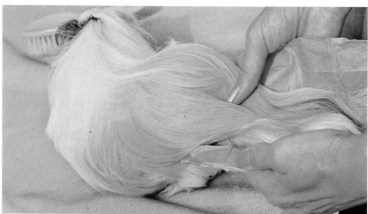

This tricolor Peruvian guinea pig is having its hair "set" after its bath.

Grooming

Your guinea pig's coat should be full and lustrous, no matter what the breed. An occasional teaspoonful of vitamin E, linseed, or cod liver oil added to the food will enhance the body and shine. Even petting improves the condition because the oils from your palm act as a natural moisturizer.

American and Abyssinian guinea pigs manage well with simple grooming techniques. Regular brushing with a toothbrush or a soft bristle brush removes knots and tangles. Never use a plastic comb or a stiff brush.

A Peruvian's long hair demands more care. It needs to be brushed every day, and a shampoo and set is required monthly to keep the fur in prime condition.

Bathing

Since guinea pigs are self-cleaners by nature, they do not require regular scrubbing. Only if your pet has somehow gotten greasy or smelly because you have not changed the bedding routinely does it need to be bathed.

Half fill a small bowl, bucket, or sink with warm water. Gradually lower the animal's hind legs into the water, allowing it to sit. Continue to support the chest with your hand to keep the head above the water line. Using the mildest "puppy" soap, work up a lather, being careful to avoid the face and eyes. Thoroughly rinse all traces of soap film because any residue is drying to the skin and fur.

Rub the guinea pig dry with a clean, soft cloth, then allow it to rest in a warm, draft-free spot (like a box lined with a towel) until completely dry. You can use a hair dryer placed on a low setting to speed the process. The guinea pig now needs to be brushed out.

Running Free

Your pet would probably love to have free reign in your home. However, there are a few things to consider, and a few precautions to take, if you allow the guinea pig to roam free. The house, or room, must be guinea pig-proofed!

Guinea pigs nibble everything, including furniture, electrical cords, and clothes, so be sure that all wires are out of reach, all clothes are off the floor (a good excuse to do some housekeeping), and that you keep a watchful eye on your pet. You may think it cute as the guinea pig snuggles up in an old sweatshirt, but part of the routine of settling in a nest spot is to use it as a toilet!

Because guinea pigs enjoy playing hide-and-seek, block off small, dark areas that are accessible to them but not to you. Check out the spots behind refrigerators and stoves and under dressers.

Most importantly, be sure that all doors are closed, not only so your guinea pig can't get out, but so other unwelcome creatures can't get in! Since your pet will often follow you around, check to see that it is safely out of the way before closing a door and trapping it there.

These two little fellows are excellent playmates. They never fight or fuss. Unfortunately, individual guinea pigs occasionally take a dislike to other guinea pigs; if left unseparated, such animals will fight.

Travels

Many guinea pig homes are easily transportable, so you can happily go visiting with your pet. Bringing your guinea pig to a friend's home can be fun and exciting for everyone. Just be sure to protect the little one from drafts and chills during the journey.

If you cannot move your guinea pig in its own home, a travel case, such as those for cats, can be used. In fact, a guinea pig can be confined for up to two days in only 0.5 square foot of floor space providing there is proper food and ventilation. A supply of juicy apples or potatoes ensures adequate moisture in lieu of a water dish.

If you cannot have your pet in tow when on an extended trip, leave the guinea pig in the care of a competent friend or relative. Move the animal to their home or have the caretaker visit every other day to change the food, water, and bedding.

This is an example of a well groomed long-haired guinea pig. Which end is which?

When you let your guinea pigs free in the house, make sure all doors are closed so these inquisitive little creatures can't escape.

BREEDING

One of the joys of being a pet owner is breeding your animal and raising the young. However cute it may seem to have guinea pig pups running around, though, there are a few important points to consider before embarking on this adventure.

Do you have enough space for a pair of guinea pigs and their subsequent offspring? Remember that each adult requires a minimum of two square feet of floor space, in addition to the room needed by the young. Soon the pups will mature and each will require its own full amount of space. Overcrowding inhibits successful breeding, resulting in premature births, poor quality stock, and ear chewing.

Do you have ample storage area for the additional supplies, such as food and bedding? The more guinea pigs you keep, the larger the stock of inventory. And, of course, the greater the expense to you. Are you prepared to invest the dollars?

Is the environment suitable for raising guinea pigs? All living quarters need to be clean, dry, warm, and safe from predators. Babies are more susceptible to drafts and colds, and thereby less resistant to disease. As the number of guinea pigs increases, the less control you have over infections.

Do you have the time it takes to raise a litter of guinea pigs? The entire cycle, from impregnation to weaning, takes several months. The responsibility of caring for a sow before and after her delivery should not be taken lightly.

What type of guinea pigs will you raise? If you want to breed show quality animals, then patronize several guinea pig shows to see just what the judges are looking for. Learn some

FACING PAGE:
Guinea pigs do not breed as often as other rodents, and their litters are smaller, so you don't have to be concerned about being quickly overpopulated if they breed.

basics of genetics to get a general understanding of how to achieve your desired goals. If you raise guinea pigs for use as pets, find out what variety is most popular and most demanded in the marketplace. After all, you want to be able to sell or give away the offspring.

If you do not intend to keep the babies, then who is going to take them? Know in advance what you will do with the pups once they are weaned. Each guinea pig is entitled to a suitable home, one where it will be loved and cared for properly. A guinea pig certainly makes an unusual gift, but you must be sure if such a pet is desired in the chosen household. Speak to friends and relatives, or make an arrangement with a local pet shop dealer to sell your guinea pigs.

The goal of any breeder is to produce the best animal possible. Therefore, you must begin right away with good stock because all pups are merely the culmination of their guinea pig ancestors. If you breed poor stock, it will take several generations simply to bring the quality of the guinea pigs up to acceptable breeding standards.

This Dalmatian sow keeps a watchful eye on her litter of three pups.

Breeding

Guinea Pig Reproduction

About the sixty-eighth day of her life, a female guinea pig begins her estrous cycle. She is receptive to a male, or "in heat," the first six to fifteen hours. This cycle repeats itself every sixteen to nineteen days if fertilization does not occur.

A male is sexually mature around two months of age

These Silver **Agouti** cavy pups will soon be weaned and eating solid food. They should have pellets, greens and water by the time they are twenty days old.

and may be bred at this time. A female, although fertile at ten weeks, should not mate until she is at least twelve weeks old. Permitting her to breed too early may stunt her growth, cause premature labor, and result in small and weak young. The first pregnancy should be before five months of age while her pelvis is still only partially fused. The birth process is then less stressful because of the disunion of the bone.

Newborn guinea pig pups will be dry and scampering around the cage within an hour of birth.

Guinea pigs may be bred as a monogamous pair — a union of one boar to one sow. Or, you may prefer a polygamous breeding group consisting of several sows to one boar. (The most successful ratio is 3:1.) Be sure never to have more than one male in a cage as severe fighting may break out. Groups also require plenty of room to prevent ear chewing and trampling of the young.

Guinea pigs are not as sexually productive as their rodent relatives. Their litters are smaller, fewer, and further apart. Surprisingly, it can take several weeks, or even months, for a pair of guinea pigs to mate. Once impregnated, a sow will

swell almost immediately. She carries about sixty-eight days, giving birth to from one to nine pups. The average litter size is three.

Some breeders allow a boar and sow to remain together throughout the entire pregnancy, birth, and weaning since a male is not intentionally harmful to the mother or the pups. However, in a polygamous group, a youngster might get trampled as a boar attempts to mate with other sows or the sow that just delivered. (Six to eight hours after delivery the new mother is in heat and can become pregnant again.) To avoid injury to the babies, a pregnant sow can be removed a few days before the birth. Unfortunately, some females are unhappy in their new, unfamiliar surroundings and abort. Being raised in the group has some advantages for the pups. A nursing female will feed any of the young, whether they are hers or not. In this way all the babies are ensured adequate nourishment. If you want to prevent a brand new mother from becoming pregnant, simply remove the boar for the few hours that the female is fertile.

These pups will be able to eat solid food within three days and will need some soft food, like milk-soaked bran bread.

Since birth can happen any time of the day or night, don't be surprised if the pups seem to "appear" when you aren't looking. If you are present at the time, remove any still-births before the parents devour the dead.

The newborn guinea pigs weigh between two and a half and four ounces, with the males being slightly stockier than the females. They are born fully furred, with a complete set of teeth, and able to see and hear. The pups will be scampering around the cage floor within an hour of their birth. In two or three days they will be on solid food, yet should continue to nurse for a minimum of twenty days.

Check to see that the pellets, greens, and water are well within the reach of the pups. Separate dishes may have to be set up for them if they cannot gain access to the adult containers. At this time it is recommended that some soft foods, such as milk-soaked bran bread or water-soaked alfalfa hay, be provided.

In five to six weeks the youngsters will be completely weaned. They will gain one-sixth of an ounce every day for two months, weighing twelve to fourteen ounces at the end of this time. (To preclude mating and fighting, six to eight weeks is the time to separate the sexes.) Around five months, the offspring will be mature, the males weighing twenty-five ounces and the females twenty-three ounces. Both sexes continue to grow until they are fifteen months old. When fully developed, females weigh twenty-eight ounces and males thirty-three ounces.

Guinea pigs should be bred no more than four times a year to prevent overbreeding. Allow a sow a week or two of rest after weaning to replenish her system. After four years of age, neither males nor females are in prime breeding condition. Old and rundown parents give birth to inferior offspring.

Breeding Disorders

Premature births: mother too young, weak, or fat; overcrowding; damp and dirty conditions; lack of Vitamin E; overbreeding.

Stillbirths: large fetuses; difficult labor.

Infertility: poor health of parents; insufficient Vitamin E; parents too old or too young; genetic defect.

Breeding

Hand-rearing

Guinea pigs usually don't need any help raising their young, but sometimes an unusual situation develops. Because of death or illness, a sow may be incapable of taking proper care of her pups. Or, if the litter size exceeds three, the weanlings may not receive enough nourishment because a sow has only one pair of mammary glands.

You can supplement the babies' diet with milk powder and warm milk, or diluted evaporated milk fed from an eyedropper. To prevent choking, do not squeeze the liquid into a youngster's mouth but allow the guinea pig to lap at the end of the tube. Clean the face with a soft cloth to remove any excess solution because dried milk around the mouth can be irritating and cause sores.

Ideally, the milk formula should be administered every two hours around the clock for a week.

After the first couple of days on the liquid diet, offer the guinea pig pups greens, pellets, soft foods, and water.

Cavies learn to use the water bottle very easily. This one has a metal tube that prevents nibbling.

Guinea pigs are hardy animals, so a conscientious owner will probably never have to deal with the ailments listed in this chapter. Most problems can be linked to poor feeding and improper care. Since an ounce of prevention is worth a pound of cure, following these few simple guidelines will certainly circumvent a host of disorders.

AILMENTS

1. Select only healthy animals.
2. Keep cages and accessories clean.
3. Protect against falls and predators.
4. Feed a balanced diet.
5. Provide plenty of space.
6. Do not overbreed.

A guinea pig that is listless, huddles in a corner, loses weight, secretes a watery discharge from the eyes or nostrils, appears bloated, or has a dull coat should be checked for disease. Consult the foregoing guidelines to see that all the criteria are being met. If you cannot determine the cause and remedy the situation yourself, do not hesitate to call the veterinarian.

Colds

Respiratory ailments are recognized by coughing, sneezing, labored breathing, and possibly watery eyes and a runny nose. They are commonly the result of changes in temperature, humidity, or ventilation. Place a cloth or plastic drape over the cage to block drafts and keep in warmth. A vaporizer keeps the air moist.

Diarrhea

Probably the most common ailment, diarrhea is typically caused by the consumption of too many green foods or spoiled foods. Withhold all greens until the stool is normal.

FACING PAGE:
A healthy guinea pig is bright-eyed and alert with a full, shiny coat.

Constipation

A rare occurrence in guinea pigs. Be sure your pet has a constant supply of fresh water and greens. Feed it a little apple peel or olive oil to remedy the situation.

Cuts and Wounds

Rinse the infected area with antibacterial soap or a solution of warm water and salt. Apply a mild antiseptic.

Falls

Broken bones and concussions often accompany a fall. Consult a veterinarian for advice.

Lice and Mites

These parasites live on the skin, causing a guinea pig

Like all other rodents, guinea pigs have continually growing incisors that are worn down by chewing.

to scratch and appear uncomfortable. Purchase a pesticidal agent at a pet shop. Be selective about the preparation that you use because guinea pigs are very sensitive to chemicals.

Ailments

Fleas and Ticks

Use a commercial preparation designed for cats, as those for dogs may have more toxic ingredients. Change the bedding and disinfect the cage.

This beautiful, obviously healthy long-haired guinea pig is a champion—and knows it!

Coccidiosis

Spread through contaminated food, coccidiosis is caused by a protozoan parasite that lives in the intestines. The signs are diarrhea, listlessness, and loss of appetite. Spores are eliminated in the droppings; consequently, as the guinea pig licks its feet (as all rodents do), the animal becomes infected or reinfected. Therefore, sanitary conditions are mandatory.

Change the bedding as soon as it becomes soiled and, if possible, utilize a wire screen bottom to permit fecal material to drop to the cage bottom. The veterinarian will prescribe a suitable medication.

Ringworm

This is a fungal infection of the skin which causes small, dark spots around the eyes and on other parts of the body. To treat ringworm successfully, consult a veterinarian.

Scurvy (Vitamin C Deficiency)

Signs of scurvy are an unsteady gait, pain, and loss of condition. Although guinea pig pellets contain Vitamin C, its effectiveness is doubtful after eight weeks. For this reason, fruits and vegetables high in this vitamin should supplement the diet. Liquid vitamins can also be added to the drinking water.

The Aged Guinea Pig

Your guinea pig will probably be around quite a few years. In extreme old age, it may experience stiffness, loss of hearing and vision, and internal disorders. Your pet will require more rest and tender loving care.

The elderly guinea pig may become less adaptive to changes in the environment and food. Even though you have developed a soft spot for it in your heart, if your guinea pig experiences pain or discomfort the humane thing to do is to put it to sleep and free it from misery.

FACING PAGE:
This fortunate young man can look forward to many hours of pleasure with his fascinating pet guinea pig.

The following books by T.F.H. Publications are available at pet shops and book stores everywhere.

GUINEA PIGS: A Complete Introduction—
by Margaret Elward
Hardcover CO-038;
ISBN 0-86622-366-5
Paperback CO-038S;
ISBN 0-86622-383-5

SUGGESTED READING

Guinea pigs make great pets if you know how to care for them properly. This book will teach readers everything they should know about caring for their lovable little pets. It covers every topic of importance from housing, breeding, feeding, health and care plus many more; all covered in good detail.

GUINEA PIGS—by Kay Ragland
KW-016; ISBN 0-87666-925-9
This highly colorful new book is a primary information resource containing excellent advice on housing, feeding and care of guinea pigs. Guidelines are listed for those who wish to exhibit their guinea pigs at pet stock shows.

BREEDING GUINEA PIGS—by J. Axelrod
KW-073; ISBN 0-87666-929-1
Hardcover, 5½ x 8″, 96 pages
Letting its readers know the best way to breed guinea pigs is the purpose of this book, and it succeeds admirably. Easy to read and easy to learn from, this book puts its good advice in a form that even a novice can understand and profit from.

GUINEA PIGS FOR BEGINNERS—by Mervin F. Roberts
M-541; ISBN 0-87666-198-3
Full-color and black and white photos.
5½ x 8″, 80 pages soft cover
For anyone who has or is considering owning guinea pigs as pets, this book offers very practical advice about keeping and caring for your pet in good health for many years.

Index